Anti-Money Laundering: What You Need to Know

UK banking edition

Susan Grossey

ISBN: 1497383498
ISBN-13: 978-1497383494

Illustrations by Chris Priestley

Susan's blog:
www.ihatemoneylaundering.wordpress.com

Susan's website:
www.thinkingaboutcrime.com

Susan's other books:
📖 "Money Laundering: A Training Strategy"
📖 "The Money Laundering Officer's Practical Handbook",
2006-2017
📖 "Anti-Money Laundering: A Guide for the Non-
Executive Director", editions for UK, Guernsey, Jersey,
Isle of Man and International
📖 "Fatal Forgery", "The Man in the Canary Waistcoat",
"Worm in the Blossom" and "Portraits of Pretence" –
historical financial crime novels

Susan's e-books:
"Suspicious Activity: The Adventures of an MLRO",
Parts 1 to 6

DEDICATION

To Trevor Millington OBE (1958-2012):
a leading light and tireless campaigner in the world of
asset forfeiture and proceeds of crime legislation

CONTENTS

ACKNOWLEDGMENTS

Thanks firstly to all the bank staff who asked me the questions that form the basis of this book.

Thanks then to Paul who said, "You know what? You should write a book about it."

And lastly, thanks to all the fantastic MLROs, compliance officers, regulators and law enforcement agents who – over the many years I have worked in AML – have taught me pretty much everything I know.

INTRODUCTION

This short book is intended to provide anyone who works in a bank in the United Kingdom with an understanding of what money laundering is, why it matters so much, and what is being done in the UK and elsewhere to protect the banking sector from contamination by criminal money.

It is not intended to take the place of your in-house anti-money laundering policy and procedures, which have been written specifically for your bank, but rather to put them into context and to explain why they are so vital – and why we ask you to do your very best to abide by them and implement them on a daily basis.

You are not expected to have an in-depth knowledge of money laundering and terrorist financing and their prevention and detection: having such in-depth knowledge is the job of your Money Laundering Reporting Officer. However, he can only do his job properly with your help, and this book will explain to you where his responsibility ends and yours begins, and how you can work together to safeguard yourselves, your bank and the financial system.

1 WHAT IS MONEY LAUNDERING?

The definition of money laundering is very simple: money laundering is the process by which criminals attempt to conceal the fact that their assets have come from crime.

Criminals are keen to do this because legislation is in place around the world to ensure that if someone is convicted of a crime, their proceeds of crime can be confiscated by the authorities – this is known as criminal forfeiture. Many jurisdictions (including the UK) now also have a civil forfeiture regime, which means that if someone is suspected of criminality but has yet to be charged or convicted, the authorities can apply to the courts to have that person's assets seized on the grounds that there is no legitimate provenance or explanation for them and therefore they must be the proceeds of crime. Fully aware of this, criminals want to disguise their proceeds of crime and put them beyond the reach of forfeiture.

What makes it difficult is that there is an infinite number of ways in which criminals can do this, and there is no typical money laundering scheme. However, it is generally accepted that there are different stages in the money laundering process, and the most common of these are:

Placement: In this initial stage, the criminal puts (or places) his criminal assets into the financial sector. At this point these assets are usually cash, and so the most vulnerable at this stage are those institutions that accept cash, such as retail banks, bureaux de change and casinos. (Also at risk are those of your customers who accept cash, such as those already mentioned, plus businesses like taxi firms, hairdressers, takeaway food outlets and tanning salons.) However, not all money laundering requires this initial placement stage, as some crimes (such as tax evasion, corruption and many frauds) involve misappropriating assets that are already in the financial system. It would therefore be wrong to think if your bank does not accept cash it cannot be used for money laundering.

Layering: The layering stage is when criminals move their assets around within the financial sector – moving them between accounts and financial products, between institutions and between jurisdictions – in order to make them hard to follow. Their goal is to make it difficult to find the assets and then, if they are found, to make it vexatious to seize them. Any institution that moves value around in any form is at risk of being used for layering purposes. Particularly useful to launderers are those institutions that can move value internationally – as can most banks – as this allows the criminal to take advantage of differing jurisdictional standards of AML legislation and the slow pace of international financial investigations.

Integration: The final stage of money laundering is integration, when the criminal decides that his assets now look clean enough for him to bring them back into the legitimate economy so that he can use them as he wishes. Any institution that facilitates "conversion" of any sort – such as a bank balance being turned into a property, or shares being turned into a bank balance, or an inheritance being subsumed into a trust – could be used to help with integration.

Although it is useful to understand and recognise these terms, it is rarely crucial to know whether you have been duped into layering the criminal's money or integrating it – as far as the law is concerned, it is all money laundering. Reading case studies can be helpful (some are given in the later chapter on *Red flags and case studies*), as they show you just how creative criminals can be and how the banking sector can be targeted by them, but the best definition to keep in mind is that first one: money laundering is how criminals try to make their criminal proceeds look legal.

It is also important to remember that, in their quest to look clean, criminals need to build a cover story. They have to make themselves look and sound like, for instance, legitimate businessmen or beneficiaries of a will or big winners at a casino; after all, if they are to make people believe that their assets are not criminal, they need to have a good alternative explanation. And one way they create and maintain this alternative (false) explanation is by associating with, and profiting from the good reputation of, respected banks such as yours.

So do be aware that even if a customer seems to have no desire at all to do anything that could be construed as placement, layering or integration – perhaps he simply asks you to recommend which of your accounts would suit him – he could be using you to form part of his cover story. Helping him to look legitimate when he is not could be considered to be money laundering (one of the money laundering offences is that of becoming concerned in an arrangement that helps someone else to launder money), and it will certainly do your personal and corporate reputation no good at all.

What is terrorist financing?

Terrorist financing – and particularly its prevention and detection – has been of growing importance to the financial sector since the attacks on New York and Washington DC in September 2001. Various attempts have been made to define and outlaw it, with differing degrees of success. From the point of view of prevention, the general response has been to add terrorist financing to existing money laundering legislation, requiring businesses covered by AML requirements to extend their efforts to what has been dubbed "CFT" – countering the financing of terrorism. So in the UK, for example, the Money Laundering, Terrorist Financing and Transfer of Funds (Information on the Payer) Regulations 2017 now require financial institutions (including banks) and other businesses to put in place procedures to prevent and forestall both money laundering and terrorist financing.

The actual offence of terrorist financing itself is found in several linked pieces of legislation and has two main definitions: money generated by acts of terrorism, and money intended for use in acts in terrorism. In practical terms, the first sort is rare: terrorist organisations (unlike criminal organisations) do not exist to make money, and so there is not much money actually generated by terrorism. And the second sort is extremely hard to spot because it is very small in volume: you do not need much money to commit an act of terrorism. The attack on the London transport system in July 2005, for example, cost its organisers only £7,200. However, despite its small volume, the impact of terrorist financing can be devastating.

Although they are often grouped together as "ML/TF", there are differences between money laundering and terrorist financing. The main one is that money laundering involves taking dirty money and trying to make it look clean, while the majority of terrorist financing involves taking clean money and using it for dirty purposes. (Most terrorism is funded by money that has been earned legitimately and donated willingly.) However, there is one key way in which terrorist financiers do resemble money launderers: both groups want to use the world's financial system to move money around while revealing as little information as possible that might enable the true source, destination or purpose of that money to be discovered. It is therefore both essential and logical that your bank's AML efforts have been extended to encompass CFT as well.

From here on, to make this book more readable, I will refer only to "AML" and "money laundering" – please understand that I actually mean "AML/CFT" and "money laundering and terrorist financing".

World bodies

AML measures have developed over time – they did not spring up fully formed. Various agencies have had their say in this process of development, and entire books have been written about the genesis of our current AML legal and regulatory framework, but the main players in today's world of AML are these.

Links to the agencies and legislation mentioned in this book are given in the final chapter on *Useful sources of information*.

Financial Action Task Force

The Financial Action Task Force (FATF) is the international body devoted to developing and promoting policies to combat money laundering. It was established in 1989 under the umbrella of the Organisation of Economic Co-operation and Development (OECD) and currently has thirty-four member jurisdictions. Being an FATF member jurisdiction (as the UK is) means that you sign up to their standards, and also agree to do your bit in promoting those standards outside the membership.

The FATF's AML standards are expressed in the form of Recommendations. These Recommendations are written as a guide for governments on how to formulate their AML framework, including

Recommendations on legislation, supervision and international co-operation. They started out in 1990 as the Forty Recommendations, and were augmented in 2001 by Nine Special Recommendations on Terrorist Financing. They were updated in February 2012, to take account of recent developments in the world of AML/CFT, and rationalised into the neat Forty again.

The FATF also runs a continuous programme of mutual evaluation of its member jurisdictions. Each is examined in turn on the basis of an on-site visit conducted by a team of experts from other member countries, who use an approved and published handbook to guide their review. The resulting report assesses the extent to which the evaluated country has moved forward in implementing an effective AML system, and highlights areas in which further progress can still be made. These reports – and particularly their executive summaries which outline the main areas of interest and concern – are used extensively by Money Laundering Reporting Officers (MLROs) to help them understand the money laundering risks posed by particular jurisdictions, and so adjust their risk-based approach. (As explained in the later chapter on *The risk-based approach*, jurisdictional risk is an important element of overall risk.)

An FATF member jurisdiction can expect to be reviewed to some level every three to four years. The most recent FATF full evaluation of the UK was published in June 2007, with a follow-up response report agreed in October 2009.

As well as the FATF itself, there are numerous "FATF-style regional bodies", which do much the same work in specific areas of the world. Examples are the MENAFATF in the Middle East and north Africa, and the CFATF in the Caribbean. They too have member jurisdictions, they publish reports on money laundering issues of relevance to their part of the world, and they organise a programme of mutual evaluations.

MONEYVAL

MONEYVAL was established in 1997 by the Council of Europe. Its initial main responsibility was to conduct AML/CFT evaluations of those Council of Europe member states that are not members of the FATF, thereby ensuring that every Council of Europe member state, whether a member of the FATF or not, would be subject to an ongoing cycle of evaluations. It now conducts AML/CFT evaluations of other jurisdictions as well, such as Guernsey, Jersey and the Isle of Man. Like the FATF reviewers, MONEYVAL reviewers use the approved FATF methodology and handbook when conducting their reviews.

International Monetary Fund

In April 2001 the International Monetary Fund announced that it would become more involved in the global fight against money laundering. It launched its own programme of assessments of the AML/CFT regimes of over forty-five countries – once again using the approved FATF methodology and handbook. It often conducts ongoing evaluations jointly with the FATF.

2 UK AML LEGISLATION IN OUTLINE

Like nearly all jurisdictions, the UK has two sets of anti-money laundering legislation. First it has legislation containing the main individual, personal money laundering offences and terrorist financing offences: the Proceeds of Crime Act 2002 and the Terrorism Act 2000.

And second, it has legislation requiring financial institutions (including banks) and other businesses to put in place procedures to prevent and forestall money laundering and terrorist financing: the Money Laundering, Terrorist Financing and Transfer of Funds (Information on the Payer) Regulations 2017.

Proceeds of Crime Act 2002

The Proceeds of Crime Act 2002 ("PoCA") is a large piece of legislation, but for now we are concerned only with the five individual money laundering offences that it contains.

All five of these offences apply to the proceeds of any crime that constitutes an offence in any part of the UK or that (if committed overseas) would constitute an offence in any part of the UK if it occurred there. There is no *de minimis* and no statute of limitations, so the PoCA money laundering offences involve the proceeds of any criminal behaviour, by anyone, at any time, anywhere. It is true "all crimes" legislation, with one little exception.

The bullfighter amendment

The Serious Organised Crime and Police Act 2005 made various amendments to PoCA, and the most significant of these is known as the "bullfighter amendment". This amendment says that you have a defence to PoCA's money laundering offences (except tipping off), despite their "all crimes" application, if you know or have reasonable grounds to believe that the conduct concerned (although a crime in the UK) occurred outside the UK and (crucially) was legal under local law. It is called the "bullfighter amendment" because it solves the problem of the Spanish bullfighter who invests his money in London and becomes the subject of a money laundering suspicion report because that money is derived from bullfighting – which is illegal in the UK but legal in Spain where the bullfighter works and earns that money.

The five PoCA offences

Concealing or transferring

You commit this offence if you conceal, disguise, convert or transfer criminal proceeds, or remove them from the jurisdiction.

The only statutory defence (i.e. defence allowed by the law itself) is to make an "authorised disclosure" of your suspicion that the proceeds are from crime – i.e. to make a report to your MLRO (or, if you are the MLRO, to the National Crime Agency, or NCA) – or to have a reasonable excuse for not making such a disclosure (see *Failure to disclose*, below, for more on this). If found guilty, you could be given an unlimited fine or a prison sentence of up to fourteen years or both.

Arrangements

You commit this offence if you enter into or become concerned in an arrangement which you know or suspect facilitates the acquisition, retention, use or control of criminal property by or on behalf of another person. The drafting of this offence is such that no actual value has to move: simply giving advice could be sufficient to commit this offence.

Again, the only statutory defence is to make a report to your MLRO or to have a reasonable excuse for not doing so. And again, the penalties are an unlimited fine or a prison sentence of up to fourteen years or both.

Acquisition, use and possession

You commit this offence if you acquire, use or have possession of criminal property.

Again, reporting to the MLRO or having a reasonable excuse for not doing so is allowed as a defence. In addition, you can show that you acquired or used or had possession of the criminal property for an "adequate consideration" (i.e. a fair market price) and so had no reason to suspect its criminal origins. Once again, the penalties are an unlimited fine or a prison sentence of up to fourteen years or both.

Failure to disclose

You commit this offence if you know or suspect, or have reasonable grounds for knowing or suspecting, that someone is engaged in money laundering, and you find out about this in the course of business in the regulated sector (i.e. businesses to which the Money Laundering, Terrorist Financing and Transfer of Funds [Information on the Payer] Regulations 2017 apply), and then you do not report your suspicion to your MLRO (or, if you are the MLRO, to the NCA).

You will spot that phrase "reasonable grounds". This means that the court will apply the objective (as opposed to subjective) test of suspicion; in short, the prosecution will not have to prove that you *did* know or suspect that there was money laundering going on, but only that you *should have* known or suspected. The court will compare your behaviour to an objective standard: did you demonstrate the level of vigilance and understanding that would be expected of someone doing your sort of job, at your sort of level, in your sort of bank, with your type and length of experience? Obviously, this means that the test will be applied more harshly to more senior staff – and your MLRO and directors will be expected to have the highest standards of behaviour of all.

There are two main statutory defences to this offence. First, you can show that you had a reasonable excuse for not making a report – perhaps you were taken to hospital as an emergency admission just before you were about to make your report. (However, what would be considered reasonable has rarely been tested in court, so proceed with care.) And second, there is what is known as the training defence, whereby you say that you did not make a report because no-one had told you how to or perhaps you had not even been told that you are expected to make such reports.

The penalties for failure to disclose are an unlimited fine or a prison sentence of up to five years or both.

Tipping off

You commit this offence if you know or suspect that a money laundering report has been made (either internally to the MLRO or externally to the NCA), and then you share information that is likely to prejudice any investigation that might be conducted following that report.

Tipping off is quite complex, but in essence what you must not do is let someone know that a money laundering suspicion report has been made about them. In order to guard against this happening, MLROs need to make sure that information about money laundering suspicion reports is shared on a strictly "need to know" basis – and if you personally ever make a report, you must not tell anyone that you have done so without first checking with the MLRO that you are allowed to tell them.

The main defence is to show that you did not know or suspect that what you were doing would prejudice an investigation. The penalties for tipping off are an unlimited fine or a prison sentence of up to two years or both.

Terrorism Act 2000

The Terrorism Act 2000 contains several money laundering offences (all carrying a maximum prison sentence of fourteen years, apart from five years for the last one):

- fundraising for terrorist purposes

- using money or other property for the purpose of terrorism

- entering into or becoming concerned in an arrangement to make money available when you know or have reasonable grounds to suspect that the money may be used for terrorism

- entering into or becoming concerned in an arrangement which facilitates the retention or control of terrorist property

- failure to disclose knowledge or suspicion of terrorist financing.

If the authorities are certain that the money involved is linked to terrorism, they will bring charges under these offences. If they are certain that the money is not connected with terrorism, or are not sure where it is from, they will bring charges under the PoCA offences outlined above.

Money Laundering, Terrorist Financing and Transfer of Funds (Information on the Payer) Regulations 2017

The Money Laundering, Terrorist Financing and Transfer of Funds (Information on the Payer) Regulations 2017 (known affectionately and henceforward as the Regs) were not conjured out of nothing: they are the UK's domestic response to the requirements of the EU's Money Laundering Directives. As an EU Member State, the UK is required to transpose EU legislation into its domestic legislation. The original 1993 Regs were issued in response to the first European Money Laundering Directive, while the 2003 Regs reflected the second Directive and the 2007 Regs the third. We are now operating under the fourth European Money Laundering Directive (and a fifth is already under discussion).

The Regs apply to businesses within what the Regs call the "regulated sector", specifically:

- credit institutions
- financial institutions
- auditors, insolvency practitioners, external accountants and tax advisers
- independent legal professionals
- trust or company service providers
- estate agents
- high value dealers (those who accept cash payments for goods worth €10,000 or more)
- casinos.

These businesses are required by the Regs to put in place the four tenets of an AML regime: customer due diligence procedures; record-keeping procedures; internal reporting procedures; and staff training procedures. Exactly who is responsible within your bank for making sure that this is done is the subject of the next chapter of this book.

Guidance

To help your bank to comply with PoCA, the Terrorism Act and the Regs (as well as other related legislation), an industry body called the Joint Money Laundering Steering Group has been appointed to publish guidance for the financial sector. The British Bankers' Association is represented on the JMLSG, and makes sure that the banking sector's needs are addressed in the *Guidance Notes* issued by the JMLSG.

These *Guidance Notes* offer assistance with compliance with legislation, and provide a blueprint against which that compliance can be judged. Your MLRO will be familiar with the *Guidance Notes*, and should ensure that your in-house AML/CFT procedures comply with the *Guidance Notes* at all times.

3 THE KEY AML RESPONSIBILITIES

Sometimes people think that all AML responsibility lies with the Money Laundering Reporting Officer (MLRO). Certainly he has a lot to do with it, but he does not – and indeed cannot – act alone. In fact, AML responsibility within your bank is shared by everyone.

Overseeing your bank's AML regime is your Board of directors. They are responsible for putting in place and then monitoring and reviewing the AML regime, and for signing off on its appropriateness, proportionality and effectiveness.

The MLRO is primarily responsible for making sure that the AML regime is implemented on a daily basis.

If there is ever a failure in your bank's AML regime – if, for instance, it is found that due diligence is not being performed correctly, or that staff training is not of a sufficient quality – then the question asked by the court and the regulator will be this: was it a failure of oversight (and therefore the responsibility of the Board), or a failure of implementation (and therefore the responsibility of the MLRO)?

The MLRO

The Money Laundering Reporting Officer is the "face of AML" within your bank: his name is given to all staff, and also to the Financial Conduct Authority (FCA – the AML supervisor of banks in the UK). He reports directly to the Board, not to any line manager. And he has a deputy, who takes on his role when he is away – it is vital that there is always someone on duty in the role of MLRO.

The MLRO has many responsibilities, but the key ones are these:

- to receive reports of suspected money laundering and terrorist financing from members of staff – this is known as internal reporting, and for this part of his role he is known in the Regs as the "nominated officer"

- to make enquiries into those reports, and to keep careful records of his enquiries

- to disclose to the authorities (in the UK, the National Crime Agency, or NCA) those reports about which he remains suspicious after his enquiries – this is known as external reporting, or disclosing

- to implement the bank's other AML procedures – concerning mainly customer due diligence, record-keeping and staff training, and

- to keep up to date with money laundering and terrorist financing trends and techniques, so that the bank's AML regime can be adjusted to take account of diminishing or increasing areas of risk.

You

Between them, the Board and the MLRO can assemble and maintain your bank's AML regime, which consists of an AML policy and the AML procedures.

The AML policy is simply a statement of your bank's commitment to AML.

The AML procedures contain all the details about how this is to be achieved, covering the four main elements as set out in the Regs: customer due diligence procedures; record-keeping procedures; internal reporting procedures; and staff training procedures.

However, both the policy and the procedures are only theory until someone puts them into practice – and that is you (and your colleagues, of course).

Under your terms of employment, you undertake to understand, uphold and comply with your bank's procedures (of all sorts, not just AML procedures – but definitely including them).

As a member of the regulated community, you are expected to do all you can to preserve the UK's good name and to protect its financial sector from criminal infiltration and abuse. This is best achieved by ensuring that you apply professional diligence and vigilance in every aspect of your work.

And as you are affected personally by the PoCA money laundering offences, following your bank's AML procedures is a sensible way to ensure that you do not unwittingly become involved in a money laundering scheme.

Obviously a book like this cannot go into details for each individual bank, and so you will need to read this alongside the specific AML policy and procedures that are in place for your bank.

For your own protection, it is important that you understand fully and follow closely the obligations placed on you by your own bank's AML policy and procedures. If there is anything in that AML policy or those AML procedures that you do not understand, or if you think that something is wrong or missing, you should raise it with your MLRO.

4 THE RISK-BASED APPROACH TO AML

When the UK's AML regime was first introduced many years ago, it was a fairly rigid structure. With regard to due diligence, it was sufficient for banks to apply the same level of checking to most of their customers. Since then, and with the benefit of being able to assess the effectiveness of such a regime, world bodies – led by the FATF – have come to the conclusion that we need to have a more flexible and adaptable approach. In short, we need to underpin all aspects of our AML regime with a risk-based approach.

With a risk-based approach (or RBA), you can adjust the level of due diligence that you apply to a customer on the basis of the money laundering and/or terrorist financing risk that you think they present. In other words, if you judge that a customer is very unlikely to be involved in money laundering or terrorist financing, you can perform a lower level of due diligence on them, but if you think that they are particularly risky, you need to mitigate that risk by undertaking a higher level of due diligence.

Why should we have an RBA?

There are several benefits to applying the RBA. Firstly, it recognises that not all customers are created equal, and that some – by dint of their very nature, or their location, or their line of business, or the products and services they choose to use – present you with a higher risk of money laundering and/or terrorist financing. Secondly, it gives your Board and MLRO the flexibility to devise the AML regime that best fits your bank and your customers – thus enabling your bank to take advantage of the understanding that it has built up of its own market and the risks inherent in it. And thirdly, it allows you to prioritise your effort where it will have the best results; in other words, you will be encouraged to spend more time doing more checks on more risky customers, and less time doing fewer checks on less risky customers – which should be more cost-effective, more efficient and ultimately more rewarding.

Putting the RBA into context

However, banks are not expected to design their risk-based approach in isolation. Under the Regs, the UK government is required to conduct a national risk assessment to identify, assess, understand and mitigate the risks of money laundering and terrorist financing affecting the UK. In addition, the FCA (as an AML supervisory body) is required to do a similar risk assessment for its own sector. Your bank is then expected to have regard to these external risk assessments when designing its own risk-based approach.

Applying the RBA

When the MLRO is designing your bank's AML procedures, and the Board is checking and approving them, they all need to be happy that those procedures have taken the RBA into account. They need to ensure that the procedures have allowed for the four elements of risk (and throughout this book "risk" means purely money laundering and terrorist financing risk – not credit risk or any other sort of risk), which are:

Customer risk: for instance, a multi-national company owned by another company owned by a trust that was settled by a foundation is inherently a more risky customer than a locally-resident granny

Product/service risk: some products and services that your bank offers are more attractive to money launderers and terrorist financiers than others – anything that can disguise ownership or allow easy international transfer of value will be high on their shopping list

Delivery channel risk: it is more risky to have a customer you have never met (perhaps your bank offers some Internet-only accounts) or with whom you deal only remotely than one you meet regularly and deal with face-to-face

Jurisdiction risk: some jurisdictions are declared by regulatory decree to be high risk (as in the advisory notices issued periodically by HM Treasury), while others are pinpointed by international indices, and still others are considered to have an AML regime equivalent to that of the UK – the customer's connection with certain jurisdictions will affect his risk profile.

The purpose of measuring a customer against these four risk elements is to ascertain what overall level of risk he presents, so that your bank can then mitigate that risk by applying the correct level of due diligence.

It is entirely up to your bank to decide how many categories of risk are appropriate to your range of customers, but most find that three categories – low risk, medium or standard risk, and high risk – are perfectly sufficient.

There are some customers whom you are not permitted to have at all, regardless of the level of risk that you may consider them to present. They are therefore totally outside the RBA. These are individuals and organisations that feature on international sanctions lists and are thereby denied access to the world's financial systems. Checking at the outset that a potential customer is not sanctioned, and then monitoring them throughout the relationship to make sure that they do not become sanctioned, is a vital part of the customer due diligence process, as described in the next chapter.

The need for constant revision

As the whole purpose of the RBA is to ensure that your in-house risk mitigation procedures reflect the current risks, it is essential regularly to re-visit your RBA and check that it is still appropriate and proportionate to the current risks facing your bank and the UK. The ways in which criminals and terrorists operate, the sectors and jurisdictions that they target, and the products and services on offer to them are all changing constantly, and an RBA that was appropriate a decade ago will be sadly outdated today.

If you are involved in the review of customer relationships, you may well find that you are asked to contribute to this assessment of the RBA, as you will be in a good position to see whether what your bank is doing to guard against money laundering and terrorist financing is still meeting that need.

5 CUSTOMER DUE DILIGENCE

To recap, the Regs require banks to put in place the four elements of an AML regime: customer due diligence procedures; record-keeping procedures; internal reporting procedures; and staff training procedures. We will now look at these in turn, and the first of them is customer due diligence.

> At the end of each of the next five chapters there is a blank box where you can note down anything you would like to find out more about, by consulting your bank's AML procedures or by asking the MLRO. If anything occurs to you as you are reading, be sure to jot it down before you forget it.

Customer due diligence (CDD) used to be known as Know Your Customer (KYC). But with the introduction of the RBA and the general modernisation of AML, it was recognised that the accepted definition of KYC was no longer broad enough. CDD now encompasses KYC, and then extends beyond it into knowing your customer's business and even – in some very high-risk situations – knowing your customer's customers, as well as including ongoing monitoring of the customer.

As explained earlier, the main point of the RBA is to ensure that you meet money laundering risk with the appropriate and proportionate level of due diligence to mitigate that risk. The three terms used in the Regs for the most common levels of due diligence are customer due diligence (CDD – the standard level), simplified due diligence (SDD – the reduced level that can be used in certain low-risk situations) and enhanced due diligence (EDD – the higher level required in high-risk situations).

The CDD procedures in your bank will take you (or whoever is responsible for taking on new customers or maintaining your bank's relationships with those customers) through four steps:

- assessing the proposed customer's level of risk according to your bank's RBA
- clarifying what level of due diligence must then be applied
- specifying how that due diligence requirement can be fulfilled for that type of customer, and
- specifying how the requirement for ongoing due diligence can be met.

Assessing risk

Your bank has a process for assessing the money laundering risk presented by your customers. This may be a form that is completed in consultation with the customer and then reviewed by someone trained to assess risk. It may be a matrix – either manual or computerised – into which the proposed customer's details are entered and which then calculates the appropriate risk category. Whatever method is used, for each and every customer there needs to be a record of how the decision was reached on which risk category was appropriate.

(Of course, your bank is also assessing customers for other sorts of risk such as credit risk. And your money laundering and terrorist financing risk analysis may well form part of that wider risk analysis – but in order to comply with the Regs your bank has to be able to demonstrate that you looked *specifically* at money laundering and terrorist financing risks.)

A customer's risk category is not static: their profile or activity may change, and the background against which they operate will certainly change. This is why monitoring has become so important to the RBA, as discussed further on in this chapter, and checking that the customer still has the appropriate risk rating is an important component of that monitoring.

Due diligence specifics

This book cannot go into the specifics of your bank's procedures, but there are certain elements of CDD that are common to all banks, and these are outlined below.

Verification of individual identity

The starting point for all due diligence is the verification of individual identity. All customers (even the most complex multinational corporations) are made up of individuals, and knowing who they are is the bedrock of all due diligence.

The Regs require you to verify (i.e. prove to the best of your professional ability) that an individual is who he says he is, and lives where he says he lives. There are certain documents that you can use to do this – such as a current passport and a recent utility bill – and the documents that are acceptable and the number of corroborating documents that you need to collect will depend on the level of due diligence that you are applying. All of the permutations will be set out in your bank's CDD procedures.

These will explain, for each and every type of customer that you have or are likely to get, what you need to do to meet the requirements of normal, simplified and enhanced due diligence. As well as the standard customer types – individual, corporate, etc. – there will be procedures for dealing with more unusual cases, such as the financially excluded (who may not have the usual forms of identity document) and minors (who may not yet have any documents in their own name). If you come across a customer who does not fit into any of the categories, or if you are not sure which category applies, you should take up the matter with your MLRO; this is too important to just guess at or – worse – ignore.

Your procedures will also explain about the importance of copy certification. When you keep copies of due diligence documents for your records, it is not sufficient to have plain photocopies: you need to have certified copies. In other words, someone on whom you are permitted to rely (and this will be specified in your procedures) makes the copy, and certifies on it that they saw the original document and (for photographic documents) the person to whom it belongs. If there is ever an enquiry, it will then be obvious from the certified copy who it was who saw the original document, and perhaps met the customer, and when.

Your CDD procedures will also explain that you need to verify the identity of all parties to a joint account, and that if there are beneficial owners involved (see *Beneficial owners*, below) you must verify their identities as well.

Customers will sometimes be impatient – or perhaps even downright intimidating – when you are making due diligence enquiries. They may simply be tired of providing information to institutions, or they may actually have something to hide. Whatever their motivation, your job remains the same: you must ask and get answers to the due diligence questions, and obtain the underlying documents that you need to verify those answers. If you cannot get the information you need about them in order to verify their identity and enable a risk assessment to be done, your bank cannot take them on (or retain them) as a customer.

Enhanced due diligence for individuals

If an individual customer is deemed by the Regs or by your RBA to be high risk, you will need to apply EDD. Precisely what form that EDD takes will be specified in your bank's CDD procedures (based on the Regs), but it will almost certainly include requiring senior management sign-off on the relationship, asking for further evidence of identity, making enquiries into their source of funds (for this particular transaction) and/or source of wealth (in general), and doing more frequent monitoring.

Verification of legal entities

Your bank's CDD procedures for the verification of legal entities will of necessity be lengthy, but thankfully each type of legal entity follows the same two-step pattern. What you will need to ascertain in each case is:

- the identity of the legal structure itself, and

- the identity of the key individuals behind that structure – in other words, whoever is the "controlling mind", whoever is providing the money, and whoever is in charge of the relationship of the customer with your bank.

Verification of the identity of the structure will be achieved through sight of certain documents (Certificate of Incorporation for a company, Deed of Partnership for a partnership, trust deed for a trust and so on). Again, certified copies must be kept.

Your bank's CDD procedures for legal entities will cover all possible structures, e.g. companies (public and private), partnerships, trusts, charities, schools and colleges, clubs and societies, public sector bodies, etc.

Pinpointing the key individuals, prior to verifying their identity, is often the trickiest part of the process, and you may well need to ask the MLRO for some guidance as you get used to doing this. Keeping in mind the key responsibilities (controlling mind, money provision, and interface with your bank) will help: the reason is that these are the roles that are most attractive to criminals.

The number of key individuals (for example, how many members of a Board to verify, when all can be said to have some control over the structure) will depend on the risk category of the customer, as the purpose of the exercise is to do enough CDD to mitigate the risk presented by that customer. Again, the MLRO will be able to help you with this.

Simplified due diligence for legal entities

If a customer is itself a UK business covered by the Regs, or a business regulated in another EU or equivalent jurisdiction and covered by similar AML legislation, or a publicly owned enterprise, you may decide that simplified due diligence is appropriate. The application of SDD is not automatic: you must still apply the risk-based approach and look at the details of each situation. In such cases, if you do decide that SDD is appropriate, all you will need to verify is that the business is so regulated, and that the individual with whom you are dealing is authorised to represent the business.

You do not *have* to apply SDD in all such cases – it is still your bank's decision. And you certainly should not apply SDD if, despite a business being regulated as above, you feel that it presents more than a low level of risk.

Enhanced due diligence for legal entities

If a legal entity customer is deemed by the Regs or by your RBA to be high risk, you will need to apply EDD. Precisely what form that EDD takes will be specified in your bank's CDD procedures (based on the Regs), but it might well include looking more closely into the complexity of the legal structure and asking for documentary proof of certain key elements, and/or obtaining the most recent annual report and accounts and a list of directors/partners. As with individuals, you could do more frequent monitoring, or require senior management sign-off on the application.

Beneficial owners

Sometimes the customer who applies to your bank is not the "real" customer, but rather their agent or representative. In such cases, the Regs require you to verify the identity of both the representative and the underlying customer. This is because criminals will often hide their true identity, or the true (dirty) source of their funds and wealth, by setting up companies and other structures as a front, and then using them to pretend that they are engaged in legitimate business activity.

According to the Regs:

- for companies and trusts, the beneficial owner is any individual who owns or controls 25% or more of the shares or voting rights, or who otherwise exercises control over the management of that structure

- for other customers, the beneficial owner is the individual who ultimately owns or controls the customer or on whose behalf a transaction is being conducted.

If you have any difficulty deciding whether there is a beneficial owner, or who that is, you should discuss the matter with your MLRO.

The UK now has a register of beneficial ownership, to which companies and trusts must supply information, and this helps with due diligence in this area. However, the Regs make it clear that a simple check of this register cannot be relied on as the only enquiry you make into beneficial ownership.

Politically Exposed Persons

You may well have heard of Politically Exposed Persons, or PEPs. According to the Regs, a PEP is

- an individual who is, or has been within the preceding year, entrusted with a prominent public function (other than as a middle-ranking or more junior official), or

- a family member of such a person, or

- a known close associate of such a person.

In short, PEPs are those who have access to public influence and/or public money, and as such they (and their families and close associates) are more susceptible to corruption. Recognising this, the Regs specify that PEPs *always* require EDD, which must include:

- obtaining senior management sign-off on the relationship with the PEP, and

- establishing the PEP's source of funds and source of wealth, and

- conducting enhanced ongoing monitoring on the relationship.

However, it is accepted that there is a sliding scale when assessing the risk presented by PEPs: although all are high risk, some are higher risk and will require more extensive EDD measures to be applied.

Ascertaining whether or not a customer is a PEP in the first place brings its own challenges. You can ask the customer. You can do Internet searches on them. And your bank may subscribe to commercial databases that will either screen your customer list automatically, or allow you to do *ad hoc* searches as and when you have an application or review that warrants it.

Sanctions and directions

Just as PEPs fall outside the RBA because you are told that they must always be considered high risk, so there are other individuals and entities that fall outside the RBA in its entirety because you are simply not permitted to have them as customers. It is a not a matter of applying super-ultra-enhanced due diligence to them: they are forbidden because they are subject to sanctions. In addition, there are other customers whose handling is determined by edicts from the government (known as "directions") rather than by your own RBA.

Sanctions

Sanctions are pieces of legislation which seek to limit behaviour. They are applied to individuals and organisations for many reasons. One of the main ones is to deny them access to the world's financial systems, which is done by imposing financial sanctions.

Sanctions lists in the UK are published by the Asset Freezing Unit of HM Treasury. The main Treasury list is a consolidated list of all individuals and entities mentioned in any sanctions (including financial sanctions) issued by the United Nations, the European Union and the UK itself. The list is updated regularly – on average, about three times a week – and part of your bank's CDD obligations is to check the current list against your customer database. This is done for every new applicant, and whenever a customer transaction or relationship is reviewed.

If a possible match is found, you must tell your MLRO who will then report the match immediately to HM Treasury. It is a criminal offence to start or maintain a relationship with, or process a transaction involving, a sanctioned individual or entity.

Your bank may also be covered by American sanctions lists, depending on your exposure to US jurisdictional reach. If the American sanctions list (maintained by part of the US Treasury called the Office of Foreign Assets Control) applies, again, your bank will be checking for matches amongst all existing customers and new applicants.

Directions

The Counter-Terrorism Act 2008 gave HM Treasury powers to issue directions (via the courts) to financial services businesses to apply restrictions to business connected with jurisdictions of concern regarding money laundering, terrorist financing or the proliferation of chemical, biological, radiological and nuclear weapons. Directions can be issued to specific named entities, or all businesses of a type (e.g. all banks), or all businesses in the financial sector. They will apply to named individuals or entities, or to entire jurisdictions. They may require enhancements to CDD, ongoing monitoring and/or reporting, and may require limiting or ceasing business. By default directions apply for a year, but they can be varied and extended.

Your bank's take-on and monitoring procedures will include checking whether any customers are or become subject to a direction, and ensuring that any such customers are handled in compliance with the direction.

Monitoring

Monitoring is now an integral and vital part of your bank's CDD. In fact, there are several types of AML monitoring going on: monitoring the money laundering and terrorist financing risks facing your bank and the UK; monitoring your RBA to make sure that it is still appropriate and proportionate to those risks; and monitoring the transactions and activity of your customers. The first two are more particularly the responsibility of your Board and MLRO, but the third – monitoring customers – forms part of the work of many people in your bank, probably including you.

The monitoring of customers is required by the Regs, and encompasses two activities: ongoing monitoring, and regular reviews.

Ongoing monitoring of customer activities

A while ago, reports of suspected money laundering stopped being called STRs (suspicious transaction reports) and started being called SARs (suspicious activity reports). This is to highlight the fact that the ongoing monitoring of customers includes looking both at their transactions and at their non-transactional activity.

Monitoring transactions is by far the simpler of the two requirements. Your bank may well use an automated system to do this, given the large number of transactions to be monitored, but it is perfectly acceptable to do manual monitoring instead. Such systems (whether automated or manual) work by matching customer transactions against expected patterns and then highlighting as unusual any transactions that fall outside the predicted norm. But the legal requirement is to report *suspicious* activity, not merely *unusual* activity, and only a human being can decide whether something is actually suspicious rather than just unusual – and so every unusual transaction must be reviewed by a member of staff.

Monitoring activity is a somewhat trickier proposition than monitoring transactions. As an example, a customer might contact your bank ten times in a year, changing his mailing address each time. This would not be picked up by a transaction monitoring system, as it is not a transaction, but it is activity that should be noted and perhaps considered suspicious – after all, his account might have been compromised by a criminal who is now seeking to intercept his communications with you. Your procedures for ongoing monitoring should therefore enable you to track both transactions and non-transactional activity.

Reviews of customer relationships

As well as monitoring their ongoing activity, you should also conduct regular reviews of your relationships with your customers. Your bank's RBA will determine how frequently you should do this. In short, you will be reviewing your more risky customer files more frequently and your less risky customer files less frequently. The Regs do not specify a recommended interval, so your bank's CDD procedures will tell you what is appropriate for customers in your various risk categories.

When you review a customer's file, you should ask yourself: "If this customer had come to me today, in this form, is this the CDD information that I would have asked for? Or, had I known then what I know now, would I have asked for more information, or different information?" In other words, is the CDD that you hold on the customer still appropriate and proportionate to the money laundering risk now presented by that customer? If it is not, then you must make it so by redoing and/or adding to the CDD already on file.

Your reviews should also check for changes, such as a change of name or of signatory, or of the risk ranking of the jurisdictions involved, or in the products and services used by that customer. All of this can affect the risk category that you have previously assigned to the customer, and therefore the level of CDD that you must do, and the frequency and intensity with which you monitor and review them in the future.

As mentioned in the section above on *Sanctions and directions*, you should also check the customer against the current sanctions list(s) and directions – they may have become sanctioned or subject to a direction since you took them on as a customer.

You should also check to see whether they have become a PEP (in which case, you will need to boost the CDD you have on them) or stopped being a PEP (in which case, you may be able to reduce the frequency and intensity of their monitoring and reviews).

Note here anything you would like to check in your bank's **CDD** procedures or to ask the MLRO about **CDD**:

6 RECORD-KEEPING

The second of the four elements of your bank's AML regime is record-keeping, and it is perhaps the simplest of the four. In essence, your bank must keep adequate and compliant records of every aspect of its AML regime so that it can assist with money laundering investigations, as well as prove that it has complied with the requirements of the Regs and offer a defence to any criminal charges of money laundering or terrorist financing.

With regard to AML records, the Regs state that:

- records relating to "occasional" transactions (i.e. transactions not connected to a customer relationship) must be kept for at least five years from the date of completion of the transaction

- records relating to verification of customer identity and other due diligence enquiries must be kept for at least five years from the date of the end of your relationship with that customer

- records relating to transactions conducted within the context of a customer relationship must be kept either for five years from the date of the end of your relationship with that customer or for ten years – whichever comes sooner, and

- suspicious activity reports (both internal and external) must be kept for five years from the date on which the report was made – and then not destroyed without the permission of the MLRO, who will check that they are no longer needed.

Several formats are permissible for these records – including paper (originals or certified copies), microfiche and scanned documents – and your bank's CDD procedures will specify what is appropriate and how such records are to be stored.

File notes

As well as keeping specific CDD documents for each customer, you should also keep full and accurate file notes (preferably contemporaneous ones) as these serve to put flesh on the skeleton.

The purpose of file notes is to join the dots between the documents – to explain who made what decision, when and why. You cannot entrust such information to memory (your memory fades, and of course if you leave the bank your successors will still need access to the information), so always make fulsome file notes and then sign and date them. The information may be crucial during an investigation – particularly if your own conduct and compliance is under scrutiny.

Record-keeping and data protection

Data protection legislation places obligations on your bank with regard to data collection and retention. Among other things, the "personal data" that your bank holds on its customers must be accurate, up to date, kept only for as long as it is needed, and kept securely. And "personal data" could, in theory, include suspicious activity reports.

As the data protection legislation also allows individuals to request access to the data held on them by institutions such as banks, you can see a problem brewing: if you reveal a suspicious activity report to a customer – or even reveal the fact that such a report exists – you risk committing the money laundering offence of tipping off. Your bank's record-keeping procedures will have been designed with this concern in mind, and this is yet another reason why it is vital that you follow them closely. If you do not (for example, if you file a suspicious activity report on the customer file instead of sending it directly to the MLRO), things could go badly wrong for you and the bank.

Note here anything you would like to check in your bank's **record-keeping** procedures or to ask the MLRO about **record-keeping**:

7 INTERNAL REPORTING

The third of the four elements of your bank's AML regime is internal reporting. This is where bank staff are required to report any suspicions of money laundering or terrorist financing to their MLRO. Reporting such suspicions is a legal duty, it provides a defence to several of the money laundering and terrorist financing offences, it provides the National Crime Agency (NCA) and others with crucial information, and indeed you should remember that failure to report can be an offence.

(A small point of terminology: it may help you to think of internal reports made within the bank to the MLRO as "reports", and those made by the MLRO externally to the NCA as "disclosures".)

You may be understandably a bit reluctant to report suspicions to your MLRO. You may worry that you are making a fuss about nothing (although such a suspicion is rarely "nothing"). You may find the reporting process confusing (although hopefully you will soon see that it is not). You may fear that you will have to defend your suspicion in court (you will not; that is another of the duties of the MLRO). Or you may simply feel that saying "I think our customer may be a criminal" is just too scary (which it is – but nonetheless you must do it when the need arises).

This book cannot go into the specifics of your bank's procedures, but there are certain elements of internal reporting that are common to all banks, and it is usually a fairly straightforward process:

- There will be an internal suspicion reporting form (either paper or electronic) which requires you to give the name and other details of the customer, the date, your own name and department, and – crucially – your reason for suspecting money laundering or terrorist financing.

- You should complete this form with as much detail as you can, and forward it promptly to the MLRO.

- You should not make a copy of your report, as having extra copies floating around creates an unnecessary risk of tipping off – the only copy of your report should go directly to the MLRO.

- You should not share or clear your report with your manager, the customer relationship manager or anyone else, regardless of any usual reporting lines. Again, this is because of the danger of tipping off: until the MLRO makes his own enquiries, you cannot be certain that other people in your bank are not involved in the suspected money laundering or terrorist financing.

- When the MLRO receives the report, he will start his own enquiries to ascertain whether there is an explanation for what has happened (you yourself may not be party to all the information concerning the customer, and the MLRO will try to get the full picture) or whether there remains a suspicion of money laundering or terrorist financing.

- The MLRO will send you a receipt, so that you have proof that you complied with your legal obligations by making a report – the receipt will give the date on which you made the report and a unique report number which ties up with the MLRO's files, but it will not mention the customer's name (to guard against tipping off).

When the MLRO makes a disclosure to the NCA, he does so online and using a specific form determined by legislation. Your internal reporting form will be modelled on that disclosure form, so that from the very outset the MLRO is gathering the information that he may need to pass on to the NCA.

Suspicion

One of the biggest hurdles that people face when it comes to reporting suspicion is that they are not quite certain whether what they are feeling is actually suspicion. As suspicion is an emotion and therefore personal, it can be difficult to give any hard and fast definitions.

It may be helpful to think of a "spectrum of concern", like this:

curiosity → *unease* → *doubt* → *concern* → **suspicion** → *belief* → *knowledge*

You should also remember that, thanks to the personal nature of suspicion, it does not have to be shared: just because person A is suspicious it does not mean that person B should be, and just because person B is not suspicious it does not mean that person A should not be.

For instance, you might be uneasy about something that a customer does, and so you discuss it with a colleague. (The tipping off offence does not necessarily stop you doing this; it kicks in only once you know or suspect that a report of money laundering suspicion has been made, and if you do not know or suspect this, you cannot tip off.) After your discussions, you find that you have now moved from unease to suspicion; your colleague, on the other hand, is not worried. It would be very foolish (not to say potentially criminal) of you not to report your suspicion on the basis that your colleague is not suspicious. You should have confidence in your own interpretation of a situation, and not be put off taking action just because no-one else seems to share your concerns. Having a suspicion of money laundering or terrorist financing and not reporting it is a serious offence.

> The legal obligation is actually quite simple: if you are suspicious, you must make a report.

Post-reporting behaviour

Once you have made a report, you will need to adjust your behaviour. Most importantly, you must not tell anyone that you have made a report. If your colleagues need to know, so that the customer relationship can be managed wisely, the MLRO will decide who can be told, when and how.

You will probably also be required to get permission from the MLRO before processing further business with the customer, or before ending the relationship with the customer.

Crucially, you must also continue to report anything the customer does that makes you suspicious, even if it is exactly the same as the activity you reported the first time round: your original report is not a blanket report that covers all future transactions and activity by that customer. If the MLRO decides that he has heard enough about the situation, he will let you know – but until he does, you keep on reporting.

Note here anything you would like to check in your bank's **internal reporting** procedures or to ask the MLRO about **internal reporting**:

8 STAFF TRAINING

The last of the four elements of your bank's AML regime is staff training. What your MLRO is aiming to have in place is a training programme that sensitises staff to money laundering issues without terrifying or overwhelming them or inducing paranoia, and that tells them about the bank's in-house procedures for CDD, record-keeping and internal reporting.

Who will be trained

The Regs require banks to train their "relevant employees", which may well be all of their staff. It is perfectly acceptable – and indeed expected by the FCA – for the bank to vary the level of training to match the staff, with (for example) more detailed training being given to customer-facing staff and a less detailed overview to back office staff.

It is also expected that refresher training will be provided regularly to revise key points, to update you on AML issues and developing areas of criminal activity, and to give you the opportunity to raise questions and concerns.

Specific tailored training must be given to those who have particular AML responsibilities, i.e. the MLRO and the Board and senior management.

It is a condition of your employment that you attend the training provided for you. And indeed you should take the opportunity to learn more about money laundering and about the fight against it and your role in that, and to quiz the MLRO on anything that has been worrying you – after all, he is there primarily to support you in your AML efforts.

Assessing the effectiveness of staff training

Banks nowadays are expected to be able to demonstrate that their AML training has been effective – i.e. that it has achieved the aims it was intended to achieve. Your MLRO may wish to talk to you about your training once you have completed it, or there may be a post-training quiz about what you have learned. You should not be nervous about any assessment that may take place; the point of it is not to test you, but rather to test the training.

Awareness

As well as formal staff training, you will be given AML information in other formats.

Your bank has an AML manual, either on paper or on the bank's intranet. It may be part of a larger compliance manual, and it will contain your bank's AML policy and procedures. You should make sure that you know where to find the latest version of this manual, so that you can consult it at any time. And if there is anything in there that you do not understand, or if anything is missing, you should raise this with the MLRO so that the manual can be improved.

Your MLRO might also send you email updates on money laundering matters (such as news stories, or changes to legislation), or perhaps hold informal briefings on key issues. Again, if you can, you should take every opportunity to improve your understanding of the AML effort and your role in it.

Note here anything you would like to check in your bank's **staff training** procedures or to ask the MLRO about **staff training**:

9 DISCLOSURE TO THE NCA

Your bank's in-house AML procedures are part of the UK's AML regime, but it is important to put them into context so that you can see how the whole process works. And a vital part of that process is the handling of reported suspicions of money laundering and terrorist financing; after all, although the aim is to prevent such crime in the first place, it is always going to happen and so there must be procedures in place to investigate it and bring those involved to justice.

Once your bank's MLRO receives an internal report of suspicion, he starts making his own enquiries to enable him to decide whether or not to pass on the suspicion to the NCA in the form of a disclosure.

The NCA – the National Crime Agency – contains what is known as a Financial Intelligence Unit (FIU), and most countries have one to perform just this function: the receipt and analysis of disclosures (which are often called suspicious activity reports, or SARs).

The "wrong" sort of SARs

If a bank makes a SAR to the NCA and that SAR is of the correct standard (a sensible, suspicion-based disclosure of suspected money laundering or terrorist financing, made in good faith), then the reporting bank is protected by law from being sued by its customer – the subject of the SAR – for breach of customer confidentiality.

If, however, the SAR is not up to this standard, then that protection falls away and the bank can be sued, as the customer may well be able to show that his private information was shared with the NCA in a manner not in accordance with legal requirements. It is therefore essential that only sensible, suspicion-based disclosures, made in good faith, are submitted to the NCA, and it is the responsibility of the MLRO to make sure that all of his SARs attain this high standard.

Consent SARs

The majority of SARs made to the NCA are of the regular sort, where an MLRO is saying, "We have seen this happen and we think it's suspicious". However, a small proportion of SARs are made by MLROs asking for consent in advance of doing something: "We have been asked to do something, and we think it might be suspicious – are we permitted to do it?" These are known as consent SARs, and the NCA treats them as a priority.

For instance, a bank might receive a call from a customer saying that he is coming in to his branch the next day with a large amount of cash and will need extra staff on duty to help him count and deposit it. If that seems suspicious – for instance, that customer has never before dealt in large cash transactions and seems to have no legitimate reason for doing so now – the MLRO can make a consent SAR to the NCA before the activity has taken place. The NCA will consider the consent SAR, sticking to a strict (although now much more generous) timetable for doing so, and then either give consent or refuse it.

If you make a consent report to your MLRO and he in turn makes a consent SAR to the NCA, he will manage the situation carefully for you, tracking the progress of his request with the NCA and making sure that you know what you can and cannot say to the customer during any delay.

What happens to SARs

Once the NCA receives a SAR, it is logged onto their database and first steps are taken to identify any links with existing information held on that database. Under careful supervision, the information in the database can be shared with other agencies to assist with all manner of investigations. The NCA will also search their database on behalf of other agencies, often located overseas, in response to requests for assistance. This means that the information supplied in SARs in the UK can be used to prosecute crimes other than money laundering, and to support prosecutions almost anywhere in the world.

More and more frequently, SARs are being used to help prosecute known criminals for money laundering offences, when the police have been unable to bring successful prosecutions against them for the predicate (i.e. underlying) crimes.

One of the most high-profile examples of this was Terry Adams, head of the Clerkenwell Crime Syndicate in London. Police had tried for years to secure convictions against him for his many unpleasant activities, among them extortion, drug trafficking, bribery, serious assault and murder. However, the fearsome reputation of Terry and his brothers Tommy and Patsy meant that few victims were willing to talk to the police, and certainly none was prepared to give evidence in court. And then in 2007 Terry was convicted of a specimen charge of money laundering, as he was unable to prove any legal provenance for his large fortune and fancy possessions, and he was sent to prison for seven years. In 2014 he was ordered to repay £650,000 in criminal proceeds; he appealed and lost, and the amount owing is rising daily as interest is added.

NCA cases involving successful SARs

A few examples from recent reports on the SARs regime published by the NCA can demonstrate the vital importance of this information to the wider law enforcement community.

In the first, numerous SARs from UK banks showed that over many years an independent financial adviser (IFA) had paid clients' money into his own personal and business bank accounts. All the while, he was telling those clients that their money was being invested in loans. After an investigation the IFA was arrested and charged; he pleaded guilty to over forty counts of fraud and deception and was sent to prison. A confiscation hearing established that he had benefited to the tune of £2.6 million from his crimes, and a confiscation order was made for that amount, with the repaid money to be divided between the victims.

In the second, a bank submitted a SAR as it was concerned about the unknown origins of cash being paid into an account. The account was being funded mainly by cash credits, and there was no evidence of a salary to explain the source of the money. Thanks to information provided in the SAR, police were able to investigate and prosecute the bank's customer for producing class B drugs and laundering the proceeds from the sale of those drugs. He had been growing cannabis on a commercial scale, and used his bank account to launder almost £80,000 in proceeds. He was sent to prison.

And in the third, a bank submitted a SAR on the basis that a customer was in receipt of Income Support but her bank account was also receiving cash credits and faster payments with a 'Wages' reference. Enquiries were made with the business making those payments into the bank account, and they confirmed that the woman concerned was employed by them on a regular basis. She was then interviewed under caution by a fraud investigator from the Department for Work and Pensions, and admitted knowing that she should have informed them of the changes to her circumstances (i.e. that she was now employed). She was prosecuted and £5,000 was recovered.

Note here anything you would like to ask the MLRO about **disclosure to the NCA**:

10 RED FLAGS AND CASE STUDIES

One of the most challenging and fascinating features of money laundering is that it is constantly changing. Every day, criminals think of new ways to get their dirty money into and move it around the financial system. This is why it is nigh on impossible to say, "This is what money laundering looks like". However, you can look out for warning signs – red flags, as they are often called – which would prompt you to take a closer look at something. And studying known cases of money laundering is always a useful way to learn more about how criminals think and operate.

Red flags

Red flags almost all have the same thing in common: they are incidents that are out of keeping with what you expect. The words to keep in mind are *unexpected*, *unusual* and *abnormal*. If a customer's activity (and remember that "activity" includes both transactions and non-transactional things) is not expected, usual and normal for that customer, you should take a closer look. There may well turn out to be a good explanation for what is going on, something to clarify why the customer has deviated from the expected pattern of activity, but you will not know what that explanation is unless you check. And if there is not a good explanation, this may form the first inkling of a suspicion.

It is impossible to list everything that could be construed as unexpected, unusual or abnormal (for that customer, remember – so your perception will vary according to the customer and what you know about them), but some common red flags for the banking sector are these:

- transactions of a size, type or frequency out of keeping with what is normal for that customer

- activity of a type or frequency out of keeping with what is normal for that customer

- a large payment into an account quickly mirrored by a large payment out (sometimes called a "Tigger bounce" after Winnie the Pooh's energetic friend!), or several smaller payments in quickly mirrored by a large payment out which is the total of those small deposits

- the opening and rapid closing of accounts, particularly if by customers who are connected to each other in some way

- accounts opened in, or operated through, jurisdictions with which the customer has no obvious connection

- transactions involving high risk jurisdictions (such as those known for poor AML regimes, or those highlighted by HM Treasury in their advisory notices, or those which are home to large numbers of sanctioned individuals and entities)

- transactions involving little-known, "Mickey Mouse" banks, professional firms or other institutions

- customers who don't seem to care about high fees or penalties, or who don't do what they can to get the best value out of your services (e.g. by transferring to an account offering higher interest) – we know that money launderers are willing to pay up to 25% of their money to ease its way through the financial system

- customers who refuse more suitable products or services, when those would require more enhanced due diligence checks

- the unexplained reactivation of a dormant account

- extensive use of cash and other anonymous instruments, where this is out of keeping with what you know about the customer and his business

- use of third party payments, unless they are normal and expected for that customer

- payment by the customer of "consultancy fees" to companies established in jurisdictions known to permit the formation of shell companies

- use of overly-complex (especially international) structures and arrangements, particularly if the customer is unwilling – or unable – to explain the rationale behind them

- customers who are evasive, nervous or belligerent during normal due diligence enquiries

- customers who seem particularly interested in how serious your bank is about complying with its AML obligations.

Just to reiterate: this list is by no means exhaustive, and every situation must be assessed on its own merits and against the background of the specific customer and what you know about them and their business. What you must not do is spot something that seems to you to be unusual, unexpected or abnormal, and then ignore it.

> At the end of this chapter is a blank box for you to note down any additional red flags that occur to you.

Case studies

You can open any newspaper or news website on almost any day and find a story about money laundering. Thanks to the stiff penalties on offer, and the growing experience of law enforcement agencies in successfully investigating and prosecuting money laundering, it has become very much the norm for criminals to be charged with both their original crime and laundering the proceeds of that crime. Reading about criminals and their laundering techniques is an excellent way to improve your understanding of the subject.

Robert Calvi: banker and money launderer

In 1971, Roberto Calvi was appointed chairman of Banco Ambrosiano – a bank which was founded in Milan in 1896, came to be known as the "priests' bank" thanks to its main group of customers and eventually grew into the second largest private bank in Italy. Once in charge of the bank, Calvi started expanding their operations: he created offshore companies in the Bahamas, Panama and elsewhere, and grew particularly close to Bishop Paul Marcinkus, chairman of the Istituto per le Opere di Religione – more commonly known as the Vatican Bank.

In 1978, the Bank of Italy published a report on Banco Ambrosiano, showing that it had exported several billion lire in contravention of Italian currency laws. Subsequent criminal investigations revealed that Calvi had used his bank's contacts with overseas banks and companies to move the money out of Italy and to obtain massive unsecured loans. Calvi was tried and found guilty of transferring the equivalent of US$27 million out of Italy; he was given a four-year suspended prison sentence and fined $19.8 million. Released on bail pending an appeal, he went back to work at the bank.

On 5 June 1982 Calvi wrote a warning letter to Pope John Paul II, asking for help and saying that Banco Ambrosiano was about to collapse and that this would "provoke a catastrophe of unimaginable proportions in which the Church will suffer the gravest damage". Five days later Calvi disappeared from his Rome apartment and travelled on a false passport to London. On 18 June a postman found the body of the banker hanging under Blackfriars Bridge, his clothing stuffed with bricks and about $15,000 in cash.

Banco Ambrosiano did indeed collapse, with $1.287 billion missing from its books; the money had mostly been lent to a handful of Panamanian and Liechtenstein companies owned by Banco Ambrosiano's main shareholder – the Vatican Bank. In 1984, the Vatican Bank agreed to pay $224 million to creditors of Banco Ambrosiano in recognition of its "moral involvement" in the bankruptcy. Suspicions continue to this day that the Vatican Bank's extreme (although gradually decreasing) levels of secrecy provide the perfect front for money laundering.

Bernie Madoff: fraudster and money launderer

In 1960 a 22-year old Bernie Madoff took the US$5,000 that he had earned working as a lifeguard over the summer and started his own stock-broking company, Bernard L Madoff Investment Securities LLC. With good family connections the business did well – particularly when they started using an innovative IT system to disseminate their quotes, which eventually became the basis of the NASDAQ stock exchange in New York. The company employed several members of the Madoff family, including Bernie's brother, niece and two sons.

In 1992, two people filed complaints with the regulator, the Securities and Exchange Commission (SEC), about investments that they had made through Madoff's firm, and their money was refunded. In 1999, a respected financial analyst called Harry Markopolos informed the SEC that it was legally and mathematically impossible to achieve the investment returns that Madoff's firm claimed to deliver – but the SEC ignored his warnings, which he repeated fruitlessly over the next decade.

In December 2008, Madoff's two sons went to the authorities; they said that their father had told them that he was planning to pay out bonuses two months early, and when they had asked where the money was coming from, he had confessed to them that their business was "just one big lie" and "basically a giant Ponzi scheme". (A Ponzi scheme is where you use money from new investors to pay enough returns to keep existing investors happy, all the while recruiting new investors. When you cannot find enough new investors to provide the required returns, the scheme will collapse.)

Madoff was arrested, and in court on 12 March 2009 he pleaded guilty to fraud, money laundering and perjury. Investigations showed that he had defrauded clients of $17.3 billion. He was sentenced to 150 years in prison and ordered to forfeit $170 million.

In January 2014 American bank JP Morgan Chase & Co agreed to pay $2.6 billion to the US government and to victims of Madoff's fraud in punishment for the bank's failure to report their suspicions – shown to have been held over decades – about the source of Madoff's money. As Manhattan US Attorney Preet

Bharara said: "In part because of that failure, for decades, Bernie Madoff was able to launder billions of dollars in Ponzi proceeds through a single set of accounts at JP Morgan."

Curtis Warren: drug dealer and money launderer

Born in Liverpool in 1963, Curtis Warren is a career criminal. He graduated swiftly from car theft to armed robbery and then to drug trafficking. He laundered the £20 million cash proceeds from his drug business using a simple technique called "smurfing": he instructed drug addicts to pay small amounts of cash into dozens of bank accounts and then rewarded them with drugs. He also set up a string of small, cash-intensive businesses in Liverpool so that he could pay even more cash into the financial system. In 1992 Warren was finally charged with trafficking 907kg of cocaine into the UK for the Colombian Cali cartel, but he had to be freed when it was revealed that his partner in crime was a police informant.

Threatened by rival drug dealers, Warren moved to the Netherlands. By now, he owned hundreds of properties, including an English football ground, Spanish casinos, Turkish discos and a Bulgarian vineyard. He appeared in the *Sunday Times* "Rich List" in 1998, with his profession given as "property developer". Dutch police watched him carefully – their job made more tricky by his photographic memory, which meant that he never needed to write anything down – and eventually they caught him shipping Colombian cocaine to his Bulgarian vineyard, dissolving it in the wine, and then shipping the bottles to the

Netherlands for the cocaine to be distilled out and sold. He was sent to prison in the Netherlands for twelve years – but the majority of his fortune could not be traced.

Just three weeks after his release from prison in June 2007, Warren travelled to Jersey. He was now under constant surveillance, having been made subject to the UK's "lifetime offender management programme". In Jersey he met up with another man, and bugging of their calls revealed that they were plotting with a contact in Amsterdam to smuggle drugs into Jersey. After some legal wrangling, Warren was sentenced to thirteen years in prison, to be served in London.

After extensive investigations into the location and source of Warren's financial assets (he claimed to run a fruit and veg stall on a Liverpool market), in November 2013 the Royal Court of Jersey ordered him to repay £198 million of criminal proceeds within 28 days. The money was not forthcoming, and so Warren was ordered to serve another ten years in prison – with the money still owing.

Note here any **red flags** that you would like to add to the list:

11 USEFUL SOURCES OF INFORMATION

Your MLRO is your best source of current money laundering and AML information, but some of the most commonly referenced websites are these:

Financial Action Task Force (FATF)	www.fatf-gafi.org
HM Treasury advisory notices	www.gov.uk/government/public ations/money-laundering-and-terrorist-financing-controls-in-overseas-jurisdictions-advisory-notice
HM Treasury Asset Freezing Unit	www.hm-treasury.gov.uk/ fin_sanctions_index.htm
JMLSG *Guidance Notes*	www.jmlsg.org.uk/industry-guidance/article/guidance

Money Laundering, Terrorist Financing and Transfer of Funds (Information on the Payer) Regulations 2017	www.legislation.gov.uk/uksi/201 7/692/pdfs/uksi_20170692_en. pdf
National Crime Agency FIU	www.nationalcrimeagency.gov.uk /about-us/what-we-do/specialist-capabilities/ukfiu
Office of Foreign Assets Control sanctions page	www.treasury.gov/resource-center/sanctions/Pages/default.a spx
Proceeds of Crime Act 2002	www.legislation.gov.uk/ukpga/2 002/29/contents
Terrorism Act 2000	www.legislation.gov.uk/ukpga/2 000/11/contents

ABOUT THE AUTHOR

Susan has worked in the anti-money laundering field for nearly twenty years. In 2003 she set up Thinking about Crime Limited, a dedicated anti-money laundering consultancy. Her services include the provision of anti-money laundering training to staff and Money Laundering Reporting Officers, the reviewing and writing of anti-money laundering policies and procedures, and the undertaking of AML audits to assess the effectiveness and compliance of in-house AML regimes. As a trained teacher with an all-consuming interest in (some might say obsession with) money laundering, Susan is ideally placed to design and deliver training and procedures that are compliant, effective and, yes, even enjoyable.

If you have any questions, please email Susan: susan@thinkingaboutcrime.com

Or why not join in the discussions on her blog: www.ihatemoneylaundering.wordpress.com

CPSIA information can be obtained
at www.ICGtesting.com
Printed in the USA
BVOW03s0208300617
488136BV00018B/8/P